Who You Are on the Inside

by Ellen Catala

Harcourt Achieve
Rigby • Steck-Vaughn

www.HarcourtAchieve.com

A mirror shows what you look like on the outside.
But what kind of person are you on the inside?

What you do shows who you are on the inside.

A **generous** person would share toys.

What else do generous people do?

A **thoughtful** person would help others.

What else do **thoughtful** people do?

A **brave** person would try to be strong.

What else do **brave** people do?

A caring person would help someone who was hurt.

What else do caring people do?

A respectful person would not harm a living thing.

What else do **respectful** people do?

A polite person would raise her or his hand.

What else do **polite** people do?

Every person should try to be generous, thoughtful, brave, caring, respectful, and polite!